What's my F*cking Password?

First published 2018 by Retro Inc Books
www.retroinc.co.uk
© 2018

ISBN: 9781791719999

Notes

Website:

Login/username

email:

Password:

Hint:

Website:

Login/username

email:

Password:

Hint:

Website:

Login/username

email:

Password:

Hint:

Notes

Website:

Login/username

email:

Password:

Hint:

Website:

Login/username

email:

Password:

Hint:

Website:

Login/username

email:

Password:

Hint:

Notes

Website:

Login/username

email:

Password:

Hint:

Website:

Login/username

email:

Password:

Hint:

Website:

Login/username

email:

Password:

Hint:

Notes

Website:

Login/username

email:

Password:

Hint:

Website:

Login/username

email:

Password:

Hint:

Website:

Login/username

email:

Password:

Hint:

Notes

Website: ....

Login/username ....

email: ....

Password: ....

Hint: ....

Website: ....

Login/username ....

email: ....

Password: ....

Hint: ....

Website: ....

Login/username ....

email: ....

Password: ....

Hint: ....

Notes

Website:

Login/username

email:

Password:

Hint:

Website:

Login/username

email:

Password:

Hint:

Website:

Login/username

email:

Password:

Hint:

Notes

Website: ....

Login/username ....

email: ....

Password: ....

Hint: ....

Website: ....

Login/username ....

email: ....

Password: ....

Hint: ....

Website: ....

Login/username ....

email: ....

Password: ....

Hint: ....

Notes

Website:

Login/username

email:

Password:

Hint:

Website:

Login/username

email:

Password:

Hint:

Website:

Login/username

email:

Password:

Hint:

Notes

Website:

Login/username

email:

Password:

Hint:

Website:

Login/username

email:

Password:

Hint:

Website:

Login/username

email:

Password:

Hint:

Notes

Website:

Login/username

email:

Password:

Hint:

Website:

Login/username

email:

Password:

Hint:

Website:

Login/username

email:

Password:

Hint:

Notes

Website:

Login/username

email:

Password:

Hint:

Website:

Login/username

email:

Password:

Hint:

Website:

Login/username

email:

Password:

Hint:

Notes

Website:

Login/username

email:

Password:

Hint:

Website:

Login/username

email:

Password:

Hint:

Website:

Login/username

email:

Password:

Hint:

Notes

Website:

Login/username

email:

Password:

Hint:

Website:

Login/username

email:

Password:

Hint:

Website:

Login/username

email:

Password:

Hint:

Notes

Website: ....

Login/username ....

email: ....

Password: ....

Hint: ....

Website: ....

Login/username ....

email: ....

Password: ....

Hint: ....

Website: ....

Login/username ....

email: ....

Password: ....

Hint: ....

Notes

Website:

Login/username

email:

Password:

Hint:

Website:

Login/username

email:

Password:

Hint:

Website:

Login/username

email:

Password:

Hint:

Notes

Website:

Login/username

email:

Password:

Hint:

Website:

Login/username

email:

Password:

Hint:

Website:

Login/username

email:

Password:

Hint:

Notes

Website:

Login/username

email:

Password:

Hint:

Website:

Login/username

email:

Password:

Hint:

Website:

Login/username

email:

Password:

Hint:

Notes

Website:

Login/username

email:

Password:

Hint:

Website:

Login/username

email:

Password:

Hint:

Website:

Login/username

email:

Password:

Hint:

Notes

Website:

Login/username

email:

Password:

Hint:

Website:

Login/username

email:

Password:

Hint:

Website:

Login/username

email:

Password:

Hint:

Notes

Website:

Login/username

email:

Password:

Hint:

Website:

Login/username

email:

Password:

Hint:

Website:

Login/username

email:

Password:

Hint:

Notes

Website:

Login/username

email:

Password:

Hint:

Website:

Login/username

email:

Password:

Hint:

Website:

Login/username

email:

Password:

Hint:

Notes

Website: ....

Login/username ....

email: ....

Password: ....

Hint: ....

Website: ....

Login/username ....

email: ....

Password: ....

Hint: ....

Website: ....

Login/username ....

email: ....

Password: ....

Hint: ....

Notes

Website: ....

Login/username ....

email: ....

Password: ....

Hint: ....

Website: ....

Login/username ....

email: ....

Password: ....

Hint: ....

Website: ....

Login/username ....

email: ....

Password: ....

Hint: ....

Notes

Website:

Login/username

email:

Password:

Hint:

Website:

Login/username

email:

Password:

Hint:

Website:

Login/username

email:

Password:

Hint:

Notes

Website:

Login/username

email:

Password:

Hint:

Website:

Login/username

email:

Password:

Hint:

Website:

Login/username

email:

Password:

Hint:

Notes

Website:

Login/username

email:

Password:

Hint:

Website:

Login/username

email:

Password:

Hint:

Website:

Login/username

email:

Password:

Hint:

Notes

Website:

Login/username

email:

Password:

Hint:

Website:

Login/username

email:

Password:

Hint:

Website:

Login/username

email:

Password:

Hint:

Notes

Website:

Login/username

email:

Password:

Hint:

Website:

Login/username

email:

Password:

Hint:

Website:

Login/username

email:

Password:

Hint:

Notes

Website:

Login/username

email:

Password:

Hint:

Website:

Login/username

email:

Password:

Hint:

Website:

Login/username

email:

Password:

Hint:

Notes

Website:

Login/username

email:

Password:

Hint:

Website:

Login/username

email:

Password:

Hint:

Website:

Login/username

email:

Password:

Hint:

Notes

Website:

Login/username

email:

Password:

Hint:

Website:

Login/username

email:

Password:

Hint:

Website:

Login/username

email:

Password:

Hint:

Notes

Website:

Login/username

email:

Password:

Hint:

Website:

Login/username

email:

Password:

Hint:

Website:

Login/username

email:

Password:

Hint:

Notes

Website:

Login/username

email:

Password:

Hint:

Website:

Login/username

email:

Password:

Hint:

Website:

Login/username

email:

Password:

Hint:

Notes

Website:

Login/username

email:

Password:

Hint:

Website:

Login/username

email:

Password:

Hint:

Website:

Login/username

email:

Password:

Hint:

Notes

Website: ....

Login/username ....

email: ....

Password: ....

Hint: ....

Website: ....

Login/username ....

email: ....

Password: ....

Hint: ....

Website: ....

Login/username ....

email: ....

Password: ....

Hint: ....

Notes

Website:

Login/username

email:

Password:

Hint:

Website:

Login/username

email:

Password:

Hint:

Website:

Login/username

email:

Password:

Hint:

Notes

Website: ....

Login/username ....

email: ....

Password: ....

Hint: ....

Website: ....

Login/username ....

email: ....

Password: ....

Hint: ....

Website: ....

Login/username ....

email: ....

Password: ....

Hint: ....

Notes

Website:

Login/username

email:

Password:

Hint:

Website:

Login/username

email:

Password:

Hint:

Website:

Login/username

email:

Password:

Hint:

Notes

Website:

Login/username

email:

Password:

Hint:

Website:

Login/username

email:

Password:

Hint:

Website:

Login/username

email:

Password:

Hint:

Notes

Website:

Login/username

email:

Password:

Hint:

Website:

Login/username

email:

Password:

Hint:

Website:

Login/username

email:

Password:

Hint:

Notes

Website:

Login/username

email:

Password:

Hint:

Website:

Login/username

email:

Password:

Hint:

Website:

Login/username

email:

Password:

Hint:

Notes

Website:

Login/username

email:

Password:

Hint:

Website:

Login/username

email:

Password:

Hint:

Website:

Login/username

email:

Password:

Hint:

Notes

Website:

Login/username

email:

Password:

Hint:

Website:

Login/username

email:

Password:

Hint:

Website:

Login/username

email:

Password:

Hint:

Notes

Website:

Login/username

email:

Password:

Hint:

Website:

Login/username

email:

Password:

Hint:

Website:

Login/username

email:

Password:

Hint:

Notes

Website:

Login/username

email:

Password:

Hint:

Website:

Login/username

email:

Password:

Hint:

Website:

Login/username

email:

Password:

Hint:

Notes

Website:

Login/username

email:

Password:

Hint:

Website:

Login/username

email:

Password:

Hint:

Website:

Login/username

email:

Password:

Hint:

Notes

Website:

Login/username

email:

Password:

Hint:

Website:

Login/username

email:

Password:

Hint:

Website:

Login/username

email:

Password:

Hint:

Notes

Website:

Login/username

email:

Password:

Hint:

Website:

Login/username

email:

Password:

Hint:

Website:

Login/username

email:

Password:

Hint:

Notes

Website:

Login/username

email:

Password:

Hint:

Website:

Login/username

email:

Password:

Hint:

Website:

Login/username

email:

Password:

Hint:

Notes

Website:

Login/username

email:

Password:

Hint:

Website:

Login/username

email:

Password:

Hint:

Website:

Login/username

email:

Password:

Hint:

Notes

Website:

Login/username

email:

Password:

Hint:

Website:

Login/username

email:

Password:

Hint:

Website:

Login/username

email:

Password:

Hint:

Notes

Made in United States
Orlando, FL
14 December 2024

55525384R00059